You said to me "This is your time," and I could hear your tears falling.
"You always said that you would use it to write. This is your chance to."
I listened and I knew you were right. Your tears and your voice held me to
my word and this book has become the first step of my creative journey.

Thank you Laura' Micl

GW00630977

DEAD FUN

DEAD SERIOUS

The 'Original' Poetic World
of
Martin Anthony Kelly

Volume One

Published by Illumin8 & Illustr8
Southlands House, Melville Street, Sandown, Isle of Wight
PO36 8HX

Printed in the UK

DEDICATION

This book is dedicated to all the people I love and for some strange reason love me in return (you don't have to you know, but it's gratefully accepted!) I leave room in my heart for many more of you to follow over the coming years and be added to my list, just don't expect any Christmas Cards!

First on my list of credits are my wonderful family consisting of Paul-Martin Kelly, Nick and Laura'Michelle Winston and Nathanael and Jorim Kelly. Not just because they are my sons, daughter and son-in-law, but because of the way they have encouraged and inspired me by becoming the complete individuals that they are. Besides it's a great opportunity to thank them for putting up with me over the years!

It would be remiss of me not to thank everyone from Di Graham for her words of encouragement to "Grab the Bull by the horns!" and her jolly staff at Shanklin JC.

The long-suffering personnel of *InBiz* deserve a mention, comprising of Mark Davies, Sarah Brown, Catherine Burden and Michael (Mike) Ackrill. There has to be extra-special mention of John, Emma and Isobel, Mike's children, for their service beyond the call of duty in adjudicating (yes adjudicating-long story!) and compiling my poems for me.

Thanks also to Anthony Hylton and 'Trish' Carter for your friendship and 'Proofreading' skills and a very special 'thank you' to *Enham Business Ability* especially John Mitchell for your belief in me and the practical help you and your organisation and 'panel' were able to afford me.

I should also mention (so I will!) the wonderful friendship, guidance, encouragement and inspiration I've received from John Byrne, Carole Pyke, the fellowship of LV Church and Sandown Baptist Church. The incredible fertile seedbed of conversation I've had with my valued friend Hayley Smith that has brought forth so much new material, without which this book would be half the content! Not forgetting John and Heather Hannam and our adopted Kelly 'Grannies' and trusted confidantes Barbara Walter and Joyce Mumbey.

Finally, and not least, I want to publicly thank my late wife, Alyson (Ali) Linda Kelly (07/04/59 – 03/07/03), for all of the qualities you built into my life and the lives of our children, family and friends.

Everyone misses you!

'Je t'aime beaucoup'

FOREWORDS

John Hannam. Broadcaster, Journalist and Author

I willingly answered Martin Kelly's request to read this book of poems. Initially, it was more of a friendly gesture for a man I have held in such high esteem for many years. Could Martin really reach me with his poems? Could I really break away from reading my endless chain of autobiographies? For Martin's sake, I would really try.

I was so glad I did. Over the years I have followed the success of Martin's family with great personal pleasure and enthusiasm. I'd certainly shed tears of pure delight at their notable achievements. Now it was dad's turn. Could he really write poems?

Thankfully, life is always full of surprises. Suddenly I discovered a new dimension in the life of Martin Kelly. I quickly enjoyed the fun and wit in poems about parrots, maggots and the delightful Cry Baby, before being noticeably moved by the quality of his more serious work, all written from the heart and with more than a hint of honest personal feelings. Poems that really make you stop and think.

I hope this is the first of many such books.

(John Hannam has a regular column in *The Isle of Wight County Press* and Theatre critic for *The Stage*, hosts '*John Hannam meets…*'on *Isle of Wight Radio* and is the author of *I was a Stage door Johnny*)

John Byrne. Broadcaster, Columnist and Author

I've always believed in short forewords-after all if the book that follows is worth reading the quicker you get to it the better. And if it isn't worth reading it doesn't matter what I say in the foreword, you'll find out the truth soon enough anyhow. In this case, though, both principles apply, the book IS very much worth reading and you're going to find a lot of truth as you read through it.

Of course since this is Martin Kelly's book sometimes those truths will come in deeply moving words drawn from very real personal experience...and sometimes in wonderfully light-hearted whimsy that reminds me of the great Spike Milligan. So please don't hang around this foreword bit a moment longer. Turn to the poetry and get ready to dive into a world of bright ideas from one of the brightest lights I know.

How bright of you to have picked up a copy!

(John Byrne is a broadcaster, career columnist for *The Stage* newspaper and author of over 40 books including *Writing Comedy* and *The Seven Secrets of Successful Performers*).

INTRODUCTION

In compiling this book of poems for this publication it surprised me just how many reference I made over the years to the 'dodgy' subject of death.

My early poems treated death with more than a little irreverence, preferring to look at its lighter side rather than the more emotive, serious side of death. Sadly it is a fact of life that death will follow life, there is no way of getting around it, short of being caught up in the 'rapture' that is!

Death can be a source of fun and hilarity, but it can also depend on whatever 'wake' you attend.

It must have been the slightest hint of Liverpool Irish somewhere in my very distant ancestral past that made my early observations of the subject so prevalent in my rhyming humour. No offence was meant in them and I hope none will be taken.

However, the sadder side of death can never be ignored or lost in a quip no matter how humorous the content or delivery.

We all have to deal with the subject in one form or another and of late I've had to deal with it in my own way. My God-given creative gift has enabled me to assimilate my feelings into verse that has helped make some sense of the finality (in this world) of loss brought on by death.

If your circumstance and thinking match the mood of the poems and verses contained within this book then I hope they will also help you.

Not all of the humour is wrapped around death so be prepared to have a 'chuckle' as well as a 'sniffle' and to help your 'sensitivities' I've separated the 'Dead Funny' from the 'Dead Serious'.

Martin A Kelly

CONTENTS

DEAD FUNNY

DEAD SERIOUS

Dead Funny

1 Out-of-Workaholic

Wally
Died a workaholic
For
He hated being lazy
Even now
Beneath the soil
He's
Pushing up a daisy!

2 Teachers!

Teachers are a funny lot
They make you work!
They make you swot!
They never like the classroom din!
They'll always stress if you're late in
But Fridays late
They are nice as pie
They're your best mate
I wonder why?

3 The 'Gifted' Amoeba

I'm
Only
An Amoeba
The lowest form of life
I'll never learn
To read or write
Or use a fork or knife
I cannot see my way around
And I have no sense of smell
But!
I can divide
And
Multiply
My Cell!
Can you do that as well?

4 Queen's Birthday

A single Birthday
One day each year.
Is enough for me or you.
But the Queen
Is very greedy
And insists on having two!

5 The Mousetrap

I've patented a mousetrap
That does not squash its head
But says
"You stupid Mousy
That cheese could make you dead!"
The mouse will then be startled
And as it shakes from shock and dread
Two hands reach out
To cuddle it
Then pack it off to bed

But sometimes greed defeats them
When they are drawn to traps of old
Where the spring comes back
Then with a "Thwack!"
The mouse lays dead
And cold
So to help these hungry rodents
To live
And sow their seed
Such traps now carry warnings

Let's hope the mice can read!

6 The Soprano's Finale

When I was young my claim to fame
Was a voice that made the wild beasts tame
My range was known throughout the land
Some said "How Sweet!"
Or wept "How Grand!"
I was so convinced, from the age of seven
It outshone the vocal choirs of heaven
Where I dreamt the angels formed a queue
To ask me "Could we come down
And sing with you?"

Though fame is but a fleeting phase
It turned my head with all the praise
Not believing a 'use by date' would come
For my soprano voice
To be struck dumb
I recall the day, the humbling hour
At the zenith of my pride and power
The perfect place
The perfect scene
On 'live' TV before the Queen

The Soprano's Finale (continued)

I didn't heed the warning signs
The 'bum-fluff' growth, I thought was fine
Yet facial 'spots' would start to brew
Till, like volcanoes, they would 'spew'
Their mixed ingredients on my face
And the 'emptied' craters left a trace
That was not a great aesthetic view
For any eye to be put through
And underarm hairs had began to grow
Matched only by 'those' down below

I reeked much more
Than times before
And childlike things were 'such a bore'
I argued much with Mum and Dad
My moods were happy, angry, and sad
But I knew best
Or so it seemed
And as I began "God Save The Queen!"
I could hear the plaudits in my mind
Saying "Such a voice is hard to find!"

Then something dropped
I gave a croak
And discovered that my voice had broke!

7 Hayley's Gerbil

Hayley
Had a gerbil
A gift
From 'Uncle Ted'
She placed it in a shoebox
And kept it neath her bed
But
It would not eat its pet food
It just would not be fed
And it would not drink its fluids up
Do you know why?
It was dead!

8 The Maggot

I'm just a little maggot
But
When the temperature gets high
I sprout eyes
And wings
And
Hairy things.
It's then
That I must Fly!

9 The Vegan

I went out with a Vegan
To a fancy restaurant
Who frightened our young waiter
When she said, "Here's what I want
I only want a 'veg' dish
That is very, very, good
I do not want it mixed up
With a creature that's shed blood

I demand that it be absent
Of any kind of meat
That used to walk around the 'fields'
That mooed, or neighed, or bleat!
And while we're on the subject
Of 'fields' that grew your crops
They'd better be 'organic'
And had better been the top

Of any 'veggie' food chain
That's free from any grain
Of being mixed with GM crops
For Capitalistic gain!"
Then while she started browsing
Through the menu meditating
I slipped out very quietly
And I left her vegetating!

10 Cry Baby

I cannot see the reason
Why I have to go to bed
Why can't they all just leave me here!
Have they no brains in their head?
I ate my meal right up today
And tried to brush my teeth
Yet they treat me like a little child
And cause me so much grief

Why must I have to stay here?
And sleep within a cot!
I wish they'd let me walk around
I wish they'd love me lots!
I wish they'd let me dress myself
I wish they'd let me be!
I wish they weren't such awkward pains
I wish they cared for me!

And why's the English language
So difficult to talk?
How come I just fall over
When I'm trying hard to walk?
Why can't I be more mobile?
And when I have to pee
Why do they have to change my pants?
I'm only 83

11 Paul's Parrot

Paul bought himself a parrot
To teach it how to talk
But all it ever seemed to do
Was scratch and screech and squawk

He tried to teach it Shakespeare
Well just a verse, or two
And even tried a bit of French
Some 'Scouse' and 'Geordie' too!

But his constant goings on at it
Finally made it crack
For one fateful day it had a fit
Then lay dying on its back

But as it drew its final breath
It beckoned Paul like so
And just before it 'popped its clogs'
It told him where to go!

12 Ode for The Self-Conscious

This World's not round
It's full of lots of knobbly bits
My feet insist must trip on it
Till my body slams the ground

This World's not flat or even
For its full of lots of fissures
That open up and snare you
When you least expect them to!

I seem to have the knack
Of finding fissures, lumps and knobbly bits
Especially when I'm conscious
Others eyes are fixed on me!

I act as if I'm smooth
Or at least I know my way around
And just when I think I've fooled them
I find a lump and hit the ground

I wonder if when they're laughing
Do they ever take account of me?
And the hard work undertaken
To help them walk so free

Ode for The Self-Conscious (continued)

Or are they just relieved
There's now one less, bumpy, knobbly bit
I've duly revealed to them and hit
As they walk on through life

It's funny, there's no knobbly bits
Or different sized odd lumps to hit
When I am happy with myself
And care not what people think!

13 A Cabbage White's Lament

I was just a lonely caterpillar
That munched potato leaf
But getting sprayed with DDT
Has caused me so much grief
For as I hibernated
In my silken 'safe' cocoon
I dreamt of future flying days
And resting neath the moon
But the pesticides and spraying
Did not just kill decay
It rotted all my legs off
And burned my wings away!
(The !!!!!@@xx!)

14 Beware The Early Feathered Fiend!

While you dream I see such sights
For as the Sun takes back its light
There are huge great owls that seek out souls
To dine on them that night
Where carnivores stalk on all fours
Waging wars in death-filled fight
And timid mice must live their life
In constant fear and fright

I've heard the shrieks of massive bats
Patrol the sky for prey
Listening out with 'radar' ears
For living food that comes their way
Even giant creepy crawlies
That normally hide from view
Are lost to many hungers
That would have them in their stew

Gargantuous Voles (some call them Moles)
Rise like the dead from graves
To seek my life and cause me strife
Yet I know I must be brave
For it is my lot to face my foe
Wherever I may go
No shelter on the ground for me
Nor in the earth below

Beware The Early Feathered Fiend! (cont'd)

Though it lifts my soul
Throughout my toil
That one creature feeds off another
I've heard and seen that at some births
They'll eat their sister
Or their brother
But it fills my nights with so much dread
That I may be the meal they are fed

Yet the dawn of day
Holds no reprise
For as the sun begins to rise
I need be aware of greedy eyes
A feathered foe!
A flying fiend!
With crushing beak
Would have me preened

Much wiser than its feathered friend
To ensure I meet my mortal end
Will rise up early
Just as I
To swoop down from the morning sky
And as I venture from the ground
The winged beast with one cruel bound
Will rejoice that I was the first one found!

Beware The Early Feathered Fiend! (cont'd)

For it's at this time
From tales I'm told
That I will die
And not grow old
But if my true life story
Has made you squirm
Please realise
I'm just a worm!

15 Dead Tired

If you are standing at my grave
With the thought that I am sleeping
Your state of mind may help you cease
From sorrowing and weeping
But if you read my obituary
And followed all it said
You will realise
I am buried here
For the simple fact
I'm dead!

16 The Must-Fly Mayfly

There was a mayfly larvae
That lived in Sandham Pond
And was studied by the Science Block
Of school pupils who were fond
Of learning how it spent its life
Until the final day
When its strengthened wings would take it
To a new world far away

Flying high into the air
Exploring time and space
To seek out Mayfly like itself
And ensure their future race
When they found its life of freedom
Was quick to pass away
Upon its grave
They wrote through tears
"It lived for just this day!"

17 Death 'By Software'

Let me tell you
A sad and woeful tale
About a man that grew so old and frail
Sitting at his computer
Wiling hours away
All through each night
To the very next day
He grew so forlorn
As he studied the screen
Till his face became haggard
His frame thin and lean

Once proud broadened shoulders
Now became loose and hunched
Until even his back
Was misshapen and crunched
His countenance daily
Matched his posture now round
And each passing moment
Drew him nearer the ground
Oblivious to all but the monitor view
As though willing for something
To finally come through

Death 'By Software' (continued)

His particular screensaver
Seemed to have him entranced
For his eyes moved in sync
With the movement it danced
He became more despondent
Not rising to eat
To partake of liquids or shuffle his feet
And soon came his doom
He would end his days there
Worn out, all alone
Cause of death 'by software'

But what was the cause of his self imposed jail?
That a man once so vibrant had took such a trail
Just to sit by a screen
Until his good health would fail
To the onset of death at the pace of a snail
With his last ounce of strength
For no voice would be heard
To explain his inaction
He typed out these words
"I'd searched through this screen
As though seeking 'The Grail'

For my family had promised to send me email."

18 My 'FUN'-eral

When I pop this mortal coil
I want it to be funny
No matter if it pours with rain
Or is hot or cold or sunny
I want all who are gathered there
To have a joke and laugh
Then reminisce of my mistakes
And highlight all my gaffes

For I'd hate to have a Funeral
Where you speak of all I've done
Yet filled with tears and sadness
And devoid of all my fun
I will have made a mess of things
Viewed back from 'hereafter'
So you may as well join God and me
In our unrestrained laughter

I'm not the perfect man of God
That I try so hard to be
I cannot walk on water
And no dead rise up for me (yet!)
But God has let me be his friend
Through Jesus Christ His Son
So let me die the way I've tried to live
With love and joy and fun!

19 Angel in My Care

I've never heard an angel sing
Nor felt the beat of cherub wing
Never seen their heavenly flight
Or felt their comfort through the night
And then I prayed "Lord is it me
That angelic visions flee from me?"
Then a still small voice within me sighed
"You know when one has laughed and cried
You know when one has took to flight
It's known your comfort through the night
You may not have seen the cherub's wing
But you have often heard an angel sing

You've daily had one in your sight
You taught it long
You taught it right"
And then I thought of you and smiled
The angel was in you
My child
And it may ease the pain I bear
An angel was placed within my care
Who's finally learnt the gift of flight
Where home is now eternal light
So somewhere in the heavens high
With all my heart I say goodbye!

(In loving memory of Kayleigh Jayne Hewitt 02/09/89-20/05/98)

20 End of Days

If I had just one day left to live
How would I spend my life?
I would walk away from everything
That had caused me so much strife
And leave behind all miseries
Which bled me like a knife
Yet I know regrets would follow me
To the sunset of my life

The receding hours I'd spend with you
To tell you how I truly feel
Unlike the times we'd had before
When I had kept my love concealed
How I longed so much to hold you close
Yet gave way to dejection
At the thought my heart of love for you
Would be shattered by rejection

If I knew I had just one more day
I know what I would say
All the words I should have said
When you'd passed by my way
No genteel talk, no perfect word
Would be in our finite greeting
For I would empty out my soul
At this our final meeting

21 Second Best

The glories of the Universe
All take second place
Even wonders that this world may hold
To the beauty of your face

There are treasures found in precious stones
Some valued more than gold
But I'm the richest of the rich
If my arms have you to hold

Fame and fortune may walk hand in hand
And I may purchase every land
Yet the profit won't fulfil my soul
If you're not here to hold

I may 'face off' many awesome foes
Crush them all with mighty blows
But if your heart to me is stone and cold
Where is the victory to behold?

If I'm going to conquer all this world
Exploring all from East to West
Then I want you with me all the way
Or all is second best

Second Best (continued)

You're the reason why I live and breathe
And the subject of my quest
Without you beside me all the way
My life is second best

I have feelings that I can't suppress
Emotions deep inside of me
That only by your loving touch
This prisoner is free

No second best
No second best
No second best for me!

No!

Second best?

Its just the rest!

You're the best in life for me

22 A Hardened Heart

A hardened heart will not see
What God The Father wants to be
A hardened heart is blind, you see
To what His Spirit reveals

A hardened heart will eat away
The mind and body to decay
It seals the ears to what God would say
And blinds the eyes to turn away

A hardened heart will only bear
Things 'the flesh' would like to hear
A hardened heart deep in deception
Gives God's Spirit
No reception

23 Salvation

No longer am I gripped by sin
Or feel guilt's gouging pain
Nor shall I be hurt by any other's sin
Evil's intent shall be in vain
For once my sin was as filthy rags
And my presence before God obscene
But from the veins of Jesus
Poured the blood that washed me clean

24 New Love, New Life

I caught a glimpse of you last night
Only for a second though
But long enough
For the light of your chestnut brown eyes
To shatter the darkness of my night
And remove the gloom of the following day
Bright enough to illuminate the faults in me
That you've chosen to overlook
Yet still call me your friend
The image of you is still here
In my mind but clear to me
Imprinted upon me
Etched into my emotions
Infused into my heart
So that its every beat
Carries you through each and every part of me
Exploring me and knowing me
Much more intimately than any lover could

I caught a glimpse of you last night
Nothing was shared
Nothing was said
But you awakened me
From the deepest of sleeps
And although it proved a dream
It was so real

New Love, New Life (continued)

I wanted to return to the same sweet dream
That your vision had taken me from
But I knew it wouldn't be the same
There's new life in knowing you
Everything is renewed
Better than new!
Fresh life is bursting from within me
Affecting all around me
I walk taller
I walk straighter
My yoke seems easier
I'm not bowed down
New love has washed away my hurts
My pains
My wrongs
I can start again
Live life again
Breathe again
As the air around
And about me
Smells only of your grace for me

I caught a glimpse of you last night
But it was long enough
To give me light

25 You-nique

If I could say a million words
Of the beauty that is you
Would it only take one wrong word
To leave you sad and blue?
Would you let it root and flourish
And fester all life through
Till seeds it spawned
Changed your heart
And blinded all your view
To the wonder and the beauty
That is only found in you?

Well expose that word within you
That would cause the pain to bear
Heal up all your hurts and woes
Then rejoice with God in mirth
The joy and celebration
Of the day that brought your birth
Enjoy His purpose and plan established
That is unique and just for you
As there is only one true *_____
Yes there is only one of you!

*(Write your own name here)

26 Lost In you

I'm lost in you
Lost in all the things you do
Lost in every word from you
Lost in time, on hold in space
Lost in the radiance of your face
Lost in your eyes
Lost in your smile
Lost in your acts
Your walk
Your guile

Lost in your laugh
And I'm floundering deep
Even lost in thoughts of you as I sleep
Lost in a vortex that leaves me disarmed
Lost in your beauty
Lost in your charm
Lost in a maze of scent filled emotions
Lost in the depths of love's deepest ocean
Lost in the purity of life within you
Lost in your presence

So lost without you

27 Favourite

I'm sitting comfortably
In my favourite spot
On the left hand side of the settee
At ease with myself
Totally at peace
No inner turmoil
Nor outward sign of any stress
Just 'chilled' and relaxed

I have you lying along the settee
Exactly as I placed and positioned you
When I drew you to myself
From where you were standing over me
Just a little while earlier
Your head and shoulders are across my lap
My left arm is placed beneath them
In a lovingly, supportive caress

Gracefully
My right hand is holding your weaker left hand
As if to strengthen it more
Encouraging a firmer grip from it
You are looking up at me
And I am returning your gaze
Our eyes make contact
I speak into them.

Favourite (continued)

In a soft gentle whisper
I invite your lips to repeat the question
Asked of me earlier
When you had stood over me
But before you speak
I can't resist the urge
I lift your face closer to mine
And we kiss

Then you ask
"Do you love me?"
With the same sense of insecurity
I'd detected earlier infilling your voice
Seeking the comfort
The assurance
Only I could give you
That I desire you above all else

This time you reinforce the unease in your query
With the introduction of two tears
That form, well-up
Then overflow out onto your peach cheeks
Forming a trail that diminishes
Before they have reached your lips
I release my right hand from your grip
And gently erase their path.

Favourite (continued)

I answer you, like so
"What did I do when you asked your question?"
You replied
"You stopped what you were doing
Called me by my favourite name
And apologized
Then you got up from your favourite spot
To switch off your favourite programme"

"And what programme was it?" I asked
You smile and say "Football
It was also your favourite team" you continued
"In an important game for both them and you."
My right hand was now stroking your hair
Your 'freed' hand was on my left shoulder
Pulling me gently
Gracefully toward you

Again I asked
"Then what did I do?"
Your smile broadens
Almost chuckling you reply
"You switched on the music center
Searched for and found my favourite track
From my favourite CD
And you played it for me"

Favourite (continued)

I look into your eyes
Absent now of any tears
Released from any inner fears
Now you are smiling freely at me
I kiss you gently and briefly
But impart within it all the love
That I have for you
Until my lips have answered your question

I ask you once more
"Now what am I doing?"
Only this time
Your cleared vision
Sees the gleam in my eyes
Physically, you relax
Make a deep sigh
Then you reply

"You're sitting comfortably
In your favourite spot
On the left hand side of the settee
At ease with yourself
Totally at peace
No inner turmoil
Nor outward sign of any stress
Just 'chilled' and relaxed

Favourite (continued)

You have me lying along the settee
Exactly as you placed and positioned me
When you drew me to yourself
From where I was standing over you
Just a little while earlier
My head and shoulders are across your lap
Your left arm is placed beneath them
In a lovingly, supportive caress

Gracefully
Your right hand is holding my weaker left hand
As if to strengthen it more
Encouraging a firmer grip from it
I am looking up at you
And you are returning my gaze
Our eyes make contact
You speak into them

In a soft gentle whisper
You invite my lips to repeat the question
Asked of you earlier
When I had stood over you
But before I speak
I can't resist the urge
I lift my face closer to yours
And we kiss."

28 Reconcile?

What's become of you and me
And the years our love poured out so free
How can it be that we are through
Now what's our hearts supposed to do?

It used to be they beat as one
They'll surely break if love is gone
A love that we so truly fed
Don't tell me now you feel it's dead

Please think on all that we've been through
The joys, the pains, the sorrows too
The times we laughed, the times we cried
The times we healed our hurts inside

Don't tell me now our love is through
Not while my heart beats strong for you
And who knows?
If we could just remove our pride
We'll find our love has never died

But

If it's true

We are really through

Then what's our hearts supposed to do?

29 No Tears To Cry

No tears to cry
No reason why
Our passion had to die
No morning kiss
No loving bliss
No time to say goodbye

No honeymoon
No lover's croon
No secret alibi
No more you're there
No more you care
No more the you and I

No reminisce
Of all we miss
Of all the years gone by
No hands to hold
Or arms enfold
To comfort when we cry

No moments shared
Or soothing word
No gazing in our eyes
No more the warmth
No more the love
No more the you and I

No Tears To Cry (continued)

No more will our world be revolving
Nor will our love be seen to be evolving

No sharing dawns
No noisy yawns
No singing melodies
No silly jokes
No playful pokes
No more the you or me

No wayward roam
No long walks home
No time to linger there
No lovers' sky
No nice goodbye
No more the you and I

30 Farewell

This is my time
My final farewell
I know I shan't return
But if my leaving makes you sad
One thing of you I yearn
Do not remember my final state
My failing health
Or weakened gait
But in your memory please recall
When my walk was straight
And firm
And tall

Within such times please dwell awhile
Until your tears meet with a smile
I will be with you then as I should be
Sharing
Caring
Embracing our history
I'm sorry that I have to leave
I'm sorry I must go
But one thing from life I take with me
Is the fact you loved me so

(In memory of 'Ali' 07/04/59-03/07/03 & Mum 01/04/23-19/11/84)

31 You Are Here

You're not lost to me
You are here in my mind
Free to roam in 'locked up' memories
Never to be lost in the quicksand of time
My recollections of you won't fade
And in them you shan't die
I won't even dwell on the matter

Instead
I'll walk with you
Talk with you
All the same words
In the same order
Over and over and over
And I'll never tire of repeating them

Saying and hearing each word of each sentence
As though they were the first time uttered
Extracting and magnifying
Every single shared emotion
That I can from them
Bathing myself deeply in the fresh wonder
Of every such ephemeral reminiscence

Of you and I
When we were one

32 The Pathway

We've taken the same pathway
You and I
The one surrounded 'tunnel-like' by trees
That permits sporadic sunbursts,
Angled left to right
All along its route
Which ends in a brightness
As though it was an 'Invitation' from the Sun

You were always that little bit faster than me
It would have been nice
If you'd held up just a little along its way
Then waited for me
But no!
You continued on ahead
Trusting that I would follow on behind you
And I will do

Its just that…right at this very minute
You seem to be so far ahead
That it will take some time for me
To catch up with you
I can still see you in the distance though
Nearing the end of the pathway
And about to step into the promise
Of the visual brightness

The Pathway (continued)

But, just as you reached the end
The wind blew
Carrying small leaves across my view
In that moment I must have lost my focus
For as I watched the leafy flurry
Mingle with the angled sunbursts
And glide gently, gracefully within the breeze
My mind drifted with them

Until they had landed
On the very same part of the pathway
That your feet had once trodden
As though it were a vain attempt
To cover the memory of your trail of steps
When I looked for you again
You had gone
But I continue on

Ahead of me
You will no doubt be resting awhile
Soaking up all the warmth and the radiance
Of the light you had stepped into
Nothing will be worrying you there
You'll just be waiting for me to join you
Sitting there ready and eager
To greet me with your 'dimpled' smile

The Pathway (continued)

Armed with an expressive look of love
And the hint of mischief in your eyes
You will utter a gentle
Teasing word of reassurance
Toward me
"What took you so long?"
You'll say
"I've been waiting for you!"

But I seem to be held up a little while longer
On this path that leads me to you now
And fresh gentle gusts of wind
Blow more airborne leaves ahead of me
Each fresh flurry
Seemingly symbolic of seasons
That separates us now
Not just distance

Yet I know that you are still ahead of me
Out of sight perhaps
But you will be there
At the same point of destination
Taking your rest
Waiting to lovingly greet me
And tease me and say
"I've been waiting."

33 No Long Goodbye

I won't say a long goodbye
I'll just draw you to myself for the final time
Kiss you on the cheek and whisper in your ear
"Goodbye my love, farewell"
Before gently resting you from my grip
Then I'll linger there for just a short while
But long enough to get the urge
To draw you near to me once more

For it is at this point in my spirit
When I feel the overwhelming yearning
To hold you so tight
And never let you go
That I will let you depart from me
Leaving me wanting more of you
So I can eagerly anticipate
Our reunion once more

When I've said my farewell
I'll move some distance away from you
Stopping occasionally
To turn and face toward
The place where we parted
To acknowledge you and wave
As if you were still there
Never expecting for you to wave back to me

No Long Goodbye (continued)

Some people will see me along the same route
The ones that knew of you and I
Each will explain to the other
'That I am acknowledging someone
Who is only a breath away, but on a journey
Too far and too soon for me to take just yet'
They will also note the pain at our parting
Saying, 'See how much they loved.'

No! I won't say a long goodbye
I won't stay in this one place with you
I'll move on
Living through the coming days
With purpose and resolve
Still giving you the occasional wave
And you'll wave back
But I shan't see you

Until, that is
The day my life journey
Takes me back to this point of goodbye
And there you will be
Standing before me once more
With the eternity it took me to reach you
Seeming as though it had all been
Of little or no time at all

No Long Goodbye (continued)

We will be together again
And all the sad tears
That would trace my pathway of mourning
Will give way to the joy of our reunion
No!
I won't say a long goodbye
For there is no such thing
Between you and I

34 The Photograph

I came across a memory
A photograph of you smiling
Full of happiness and fun
Before your 'trials' had begun
No hurt
No sorrow
Were on display
Just your broadened smile
From joyful play
My soul was lifted deep inside
There was no pain for you to hide
Then I smiled
Kissed the photo of you
And cried

BIBLIOGRAPHY

Copyright

1	Out-of-Workaholic	© Martin Kelly 12/12/98
2	Teachers!	© Martin Kelly 10/10/92
3	The 'Gifted' Amoeba	© Martin Kelly 07/04/92
4	Queen's Birthday	© Martin Kelly 07/04/92
5	The Mousetrap	© Martin Kelly 26/09/96
6	The Soprano's Finale	© Martin Kelly 10/10/99
	(Up-dated)	© Martin Kelly 05/08/04
7	Hayley's Gerbil	© Martin Kelly 07/04/92
	(Up-dated)	© Martin Kelly 18/06/04
8	The Maggot	© Martin Kelly 10/10/98
9	The Vegan	© Martin Kelly 13/08/04
10	Cry Baby	© Martin Kelly 28/09/96
	(Up-dated)	© Martin Kelly 13/08/04
11	Paul's Parrot	© Martin Kelly 10/12/98
	(Up-dated)	© Martin Kelly 16/10/04
12	Ode for The Self Conscious	© Martin Kelly 20/09/96
	(Up-dated)	© Martin Kelly 23/06/04
13	A Cabbage White's Lament	© Martin Kelly 26/07/98
14	Beware T'Early Feathered Fiend!	© Martin Kelly 05/08/04
15	Dead Tired	© Martin Kelly 01/08/04
16	The Must-Fly Mayfly	© Martin Kelly 10/10/98
17	Death 'By Software'	© Martin Kelly 09/09/04
18	My 'FUN'-eral	© Martin Kelly 13/10/04
19	Angel In My Care	© Martin Kelly 20/05/98
20	End of Days	© Martin Kelly 03/09/04
21	Second Best	© Martin Kelly 17/06/04
22	A Hardened Heart	© Martin Kelly 13/06/82
23	Salvation	© Martin Kelly 03/07/81
24	New Love, New Life	© Martin Kelly 13/08/04
25	You-nique	© Martin Kelly 26/07/04
26	Lost In You	© Martin Kelly 17/06/04
27	Favourite	© Martin Kelly 26/08/04
28	Reconcile?	© Martin Kelly 28/02/01
29	No Tears To Cry	© Martin Kelly 11/01/01
30	Farewell	© Martin Kelly 09/08/96
	(Up-dated)	© Martin Kelly 14/07/03
	(Up-dated further)	© Martin Kelly 09/08/04
31	You Are Here	© Martin Kelly 15/07/03
32	The Pathway	© Martin Kelly 15/07/03
33	No Long Goodbye	© Martin Kelly 15/07/03
34	The Photograph	© Martin Kelly 13/08/04

Illumin8 & Illustr8